Selma Burke
Artist

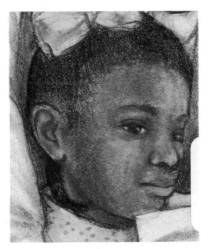

Written by Garnet Nelson Jackson
Illustrated by Cheryl Hanna

MODERN CURRICULUM PRESS

Program Reviewers

Leila Eames, Coordinator of Instruction,
  Chapter 1
  New Orleans Public Schools
  New Orleans, Louisiana

Stephanie Mahan, Teacher
  Bethune Elementary School
  San Diego, California

Thomasina M. Portis, Director
  Multicultural/Values Education
  District of Columbia
  Public Schools
  Washington, D.C.

ISBN 0-8136-5246-4 (Paperback)   0-8136-5240-5 (Reinforced Binding)
Printed in the United States of America

10 9 8 7 6   06 05 04 03 02

Pearson Learning Group

1-800-321-3106
www.pearsonlearning.com

Dear Readers,

When Selma Burke was young, she liked making things with clay. What she made looked beautiful. She soon realized she had a special talent.

She wanted to use that talent as an artist. She became one of the greatest sculptors in the country.

If you like to do something and you do it quite well, it is probably your special talent. If you really work at it, perhaps you will have something to share with the world.

Your friend,

Selma Burke, six years old, knelt
beside the creek in Mooresville,
North Carolina. Her hands slid
under the water for the white clay
below. Her mother used the clay
as whitewash, or paint, as many
people did in 1906.

The little girl squeezed the water from the ball of clay. When she opened her hand, she saw her palm print on the clay.

"Maybe I can shape a star," she thought to herself. She patted and poked the soft mud. From then on, Selma loved to shape things from clay.

3

When she was eight years old, Selma started writing poetry. She also dreamed of being an artist.

Selma's mother, Mary, tried to talk her out of being an artist. Mary wanted Selma to have a *real* job like her brothers and sisters. They were lawyers, preachers, and a doctor. Selma's father, however, always encouraged Selma's dream.

When it was time for Selma to go to college, she wanted to study art. However, her mother wanted her to be a nurse. So Selma went to nursing school and became a nurse.

Selma took a job as a nurse in New
York. But she did not give up her dream
of being an artist. In her free time, she
studied art and sculpture—making
shapes out of clay or wood.

Soon Selma began working as an artist. Even then she kept studying art. When she could, she went to Europe and studied with artists there.

At first Selma did not earn much
money with her art. In the 1930s, she
taught at the Harlem Art Center in New
York. She also taught in some
government art programs. These
programs helped many young African
American artists.

People began to like Selma's
sculptures and bought them. She
was one of the first African American
women to become famous as an
artist. In 1940, she was able to open
the Selma Burke School of Sculpture.

In New York City, Selma was the
friend of many writers and artists.
Many of her friends became famous.
Selma's art, also, won many awards
and prizes.

13

In 1943, Selma won a contest to make a sculpture of President Franklin D. Roosevelt. Selma worked on her sculpture of him for over a year. Selma's sculpture was put in a new government building.

Soon after, the government decided to put President Roosevelt's picture on a new dime. They chose to copy Selma's sculpture of him because it looked so much like the President. Her art was put on the United States dime.

Selma's fame as an artist grew. Many young artists studied with her. Also, to bring art to even more people, Selma opened the Selma Burke Art Center in Pittsburgh, Pennsylvania.

Many schools gave Selma awards. When she was seventy years old, she earned another college degree. She became Doctor Selma Burke.

Museums all over the world show sculptures by Selma Burke. But Americans do not have to go to a museum to see her art. All they have to do is look at a dime!

A girl with magic fingers—
That was Selma Burke.
Molding clay to look like people
Was her favorite work.

Her dream of being an artist
Over time remained intact—
Selma worked and worked
And made her dream a fact.

Her fingers went to work.
1945 was the time
When her profile of President Roosevelt
Was put on the U.S. dime.

She's known the world over
For all she's done.
An artist to remember—
Selma Burke's the one.

Glossary

famous (fā′ məs) well known

museum (myo͞o zē′ əm) a place that shows
    collections of things for people to see

plaque (plak) a flat piece of metal or wood often
    used as a wall decoration

sculpture (skulp′ chər) the art of modeling wood,
    clay or metal into different shapes

whitewash (wīt′ wäsh) a white liquid made from
    lime, powdered chalk, and water used to paint
    walls white

About the Author

Garnet Jackson was born and raised in New Orleans, Louisiana. She is now an elementary school teacher in Flint, Michigan, with a deep concern for developing a positive self-image in young African American students. After an unsuccessful search for materials on famous African Americans written for early readers, Ms. Jackson produced a series of biographies herself. She has now written a second series. Besides being a teacher, Ms. Jackson is a poet and a newspaper columnist. She dedicates this book with love to her son Damon.

About the Illustrator

Cheryl Hanna, a native of Michigan, is an illustrator and fine artist who has also worked as a designer and teacher. Ms. Hanna has illustrated several other books, including *An Enchanted Hair Tale*, which was a 1987 ALA Notable Book. In *Selma Burke*, she uses pencil and oil wash to present critical events in the life of an important American artist.